VARIANT III
**Allegretto** (♩ = 150)

# OXFORD
## UNIVERSITY PRESS

www.oup.com

ISBN 978-0-19-386649-2

Ralph Vaughan Williams

# *Five Variants of 'Dives and Lazarus'*

For String Orchestra and Harp

## Violin II

OXFORD

UNIVERSITY PRESS

**Violin II**

# FIVE VARIANTS OF 'DIVES AND LAZARUS'
## For String Orchestra and Harp

R. Vaughan Williams